THE MOVING STAIR

GW00566704

About the Author

Gabriel Fitzmaurice was born in 1952 in Moyvane, Co Kerry, where he lives and teaches in the local national school, having previously taught in Avoca, Co Wicklow and Caherdavin, Limerick City.

A former chairman and literary advisor of Writers' Week, Listowel, he has published several collections of poetry in English and one in Irish. These were published to critical acclaim.

THE MOVING STAIR

GABRIEL FITZMAURICE
WITH ILLUSTRATIONS BY DONALD TESKEY

Children's
POOLBEG

First published 1993 by
Poolbeg,
A division of Poolbeg Enterprises Ltd,
Knocksedan House,
Swords, Co Dublin, Ireland.
Reprinted December 1993

A catalogue record for this book is available from the British Library.

ISBN 1 85371 267 1

Illustrated by Donald Teskey
Cover design by Poolbeg Group Services Ltd
Set by Mac Book Limited in Stone 10/15
Printed by The Guernsey Press Limited,
Vale, Guernsey, Channel Islands.

Contents

To John and Nessa for reminding me.
With love from Daddy Pussy Cat...

The New Baby

Mam got a new baby
And she brought him home
And Daddy was happy;
But I write this poem.

To tell you the trouble
That baby has brought:
A baby's more trouble
Than ever I thought.

He cries in the morning,
He cries in the night,
He cries if it's dusky,
He cries if it's bright;

And a bottle's no good
To that little mug:
He only stops crying
When he gets a hug.

And when Mammy rocks him
He closes his eyes;
But when she puts him to bed
He wakes up and he cries.

When my parents had me,
They'd no need of another
'Cos the last thing I wanted
Was a cross little brother.

Lost

Once when I was shopping
With Daddy in Tralee
I got lost in this hardware shop.
I looked but couldn't see

Him anywhere. So I
Wandered 'round the town
Lost and sobbing to myself
Crying "Daddy" up and down.

And then a Garda found me
'Cos they were on the street
Looking for a boy with a leather coat
And missing three front teeth.

And he put me in the squad car
And took me to my Dad:
He wasn't cross that I got lost
And I was very glad.

Sucking Song

Lobely be suckin her doe-doe*
Lobely be suckin her thumb
Lobely be suckin her piggy-toe
Lobely be suckin em yum

* doe-doe: a baby's soother

I Spilled My Picture

I spilled my picture
Yesterday
From brightest bright
To dullest grey.

I hung my painting
Up to dry—
The colours ran:
'Twould make you cry.

Streams of colour
Fell like tears
And weird fantastic
Shapes appeared

And left my picture
In a mess
And drained my painting
Colourless.

Piddling Song

I don't need a nappy
'Cos now I'm nearly three—
I tinkle in my potty.
Come here and watch me...see?

Who's She Like?

I look like my auntie,
I look like my mother,
I look like my cousins,
I look like my brother.

Every time anyone
Meets Mammy and me,
They always start peering
To examine me:

"She has the nose of her father,
Her mother's red hair,
The smile of her granda"—
For all that they care

I might be a statue.
Why don't they see *me*
And not bits and pieces
Of my family.

My Puppy Charlie

My puppy Charlie—
He bites and he bites;
He bites fingers and papers
And curtains and tights.

He barks all night long
And he messes the place—
But he's furry and cuddly,
And he licks my face.

It's Only Simple Adding

It's only simple adding,
That's all you've got to do:
Just write the sum and add it—
It's just like 2 + 2.

That's fine for you to say it,
But you have no regard—
I think that you've forgotten
When 2 + 2 was hard.

I Live in the Country

I live in the country
And I work on the farm
With machines and big tractors
But I keep out of harm.

When Mammy wants shopping
I have to walk to the store.
(You could be shopping for Mammy
Till your feet would be sore!)

Every morning and evening
When we're milking the cows
I fetch milk for the cats
And milk for the house.

With the dogs and the cats
I have lots of fun;
I let the calf suck my fingers
With his tickly tongue.

I slide down the haystacks
And swing on the gate,
And if Mammy is busy
I go to bed late.

I'm cute as a jackdaw
And wild as a pup
And I don't care what I'll be
When I grow up.

Whack!

Mammy says
I'm very bold,
That I never do
What I'm told;

And once she went
To give me a smack
But I pulled my hand
And all the *whack*

Beat on Mammy's
Other hand—
But Mam just laughed
And all was grand.

Catherine Is a Big Girl Now

Running up the short-cut
As fast as I could fly,
I tumbled in a puddle
And I didn't even cry.

In the Class

In the class
As bold as brass
Lots of lovely noise:
Chase and run,
Yippee such fun:
Naughty girls and boys.

The Hunt

Will I? No—'twill hurt me!
I could never do it,
But my tongue keeps pushing,
pushing—
The pain! I can't go through it...

Back tongue! Back tongue! Sit, I tell
you!
I don't want to do it—
Let the fairies keep their money,
Even if they strew it.

Back tongue! Back tongue! Whoa, I
tell you,
Bloodhound in my mouth!
Panting now, the hunt is over,
Another tooth knocked out.

Charlie MacRory

Young Charlie MacRory
Has just come to school,
And he never stops crying:
He's a right little fool.

But Charlie MacRory
Is no fool at all:
He got a sweet from the teacher
When he started to bawl.

My Family

Daddy is bigger than the sink,
Mammy is bigger than the cat,
And I am bigger than baby
Who's small and pink and fat.

The Wind

I don't like the wind:
When it blows I can't go out.
The wind is a monster raging,
The wind is a dirty shout.

The wind is a monster raging,
The wind is a dirty shout
That blows me like an umbrella;
That would turn me inside-out.

The wind is caged in atmosphere
And it's bursting to get out:
That's why it's a monster raging.
And when the wind breaks out

The wind is rafters aching,
The wind is a tree that flops,
The wind is a pole that's breaking.
STOP WIND! STOP! STOP! STOP!

A Little Bull

Too much manners
Make me sick:
When I'm hungry
I get food quick.

And Mammy calls me
"A little bull,"
But I don't mind
Because I'm full.

The Teacher

I kinda like the teacher,
But he's most awful cross.
He really throws his weight about:
He sure can act the boss.

But still, he tells us stories;
And he's nice and funny too.
He's nice—but he could be nicer.
I suppose we could be nicer too.

My First Day at School

I remember very well
The first day I went to school;
I was four and big and brave:
I had books, a bag and rule.

My hair was awful tidy,
My clothes were awful neat
As I walked with the bigger boys
Along my friend, the street

Which now was filled with creamery-
cars,
Horses and asses too;
And the farmers laughed and called
to me
To mind myself at school.

And so we turned the corner
Where men propped up the wall,
Round the corner, up the hill,
I could hear the farmers' call

That I should mind myself at school:
Now why should they say that
'Cos Mammy said that school was
nice
And I was thinking what

Kind of sweets the teacher had
And how many she'd give me
When up ahead, a big boy said:
"Come along with me."

No Mammy or no Daddy,
No teacher there to greet,
Just a big boy giving orders—
And all for a stupid sweet.

So I turned and ran away
With the big boy after me
But I raced him down the hill
And I was alone and free.

And then I went and sneaked in
home
And told my tale to Daddy.
He didn't send me back to school
Till I was good and ready.

Stroking Susan's Hair

Dreaming in the classroom
Barely barely there
Hum of children's voices
Stroking Susan's hair

Long and loose and luscious
Lapping lapping me
Purring through my fingers
That soothe so swimmingly

Dreaming in the classroom
Barely barely there
Floating like a feather
Falling in the air

Upsy-Daisy

Upsy daisy doodle dandy
Daddy loves his daughter
Gives her gravy, gives her pandy
Warms her milk with water

Chimney On Fire

"Chimney on fire,"
The neighbours said:
"Someone send
For the fire brigade."

"Hurry! Hurry!"
Came the shout
As clouds of smoke
Volcanoed out.

Then the engine came
With flashing light
That cut like lightning
Through the night.

And the firemen spidered
Up the roof,
Up the chimney:
The fire went WHOOSH

And showers of sparks
Gushed up the flue.
They put the smoke
And the fire out too.

Mrs Squirrel

Silly girl,
Mrs Squirrel:
You're squelchy in your guts.
It's very rude:
Go get some food
And stuff that squelch with nuts.

Another Point of View

Boys are silly sometimes
When they're all biff and broil.
They think the things that they do
best
Are the only things worth while.

They never learn cooking
Or how to knit or sew.
They think the things that they do
best
Are the only things to know.

Now Daddy is much better
And he knows things people should:
He even cooks the dinner,
And although it's not too good

It's better to have scorched bacon
And eggs that are burnt to cinder
Than to starve for want of cooking
And have nothing for your dinner.

My Daddy

My Daddy is always on the phone;
He gets lots of letters too;
My Daddy is very busy:
He has lots of things to do.

My Daddy is very funny,
But sometimes he gets mad;
My Daddy gives me money;
Sometimes I help my Dad.

My Daddy's name is Eddie
And he can be very kind.
My Daddy is often away from home
But I don't really mind

Because I know he loves us
And we all love him too.
My Daddy has no hair;
My Dad can make a stew.

29

My Daddy sows the garden;
My Daddy mows the lawn;
My Daddy puts me up to bed
When I yawn;

And he tells me bedtime stories;
He hugs me when I'm sad;
He gives me a birthday present—
I love my Dad.

The Lady

The lady in the house *ahind*
Is cold and blue and tall;
She never moves around the room
And never talks at all.

She crushes the black serpent
'Cos he is very bold—
She'll crush me too, my Granda says,
If I don't do what I'm told.

We're building a big grotto,
Billy Quirke and me—
He hammers at these great big stones
But stops and talks to me.

We're taking out the lady
After lunch today—
We'll put her in the grotto
And there she'll have to stay.

Snow

A cold, dark evening:
I should be in I know,
But here it comes falling—
SNOW! SNOW! SNOW!

I let it fall upon my head,
Into my mouth and eyes:
I'm glad when snow is falling
For it's always a surprise.

Whiteness, brightness everywhere:
I love the white, and yet
I love the slushy puddles
When the snow is turning wet.

My Dream

Once I had a dream
That Christmastime was here,
That Santa Claus had come to me
And taken cake and beer;

And I woke up full of glee,
Then, jumping out of bed,
I ran to get my presents—
"It's Christmas Day!" I said.

But Mammy in the kitchen called
"You'll be late for school—
It's the middle of September."
Waking up is cruel...

A Footballer
For Kieran Byrne

I'm not too good at football,
And I wouldn't get my place
On any top-class football team,
But that's no great disgrace.

You see—every time I chase the ball
Someone always gets there first,
And every game I play in,
I'm always about the worst.

I've practised at my shooting—
I've tried and tried and tried,
But every time I take a kick,
It always ends up wide.

And though I'm a better jumper
Than most of the other boys,
Every time I'm in the air
I always close my eyes.

Oh to be on the 'A' team
And to hear the crowd's hubbub,
And be cheered and clapped and
screeched at—
Even to be a sub.

But I'll always be on the sideline,
Still there's one thing I can do—
I can cheer them sometimes.
I suppose that's what I'll do.

I Thought a Fish Had Wings

I thought a fish had wings;
And then one day at school
I said a fish swam with his wings.
I felt an awful fool:

The boys and girls laughed out so
loud
That I turned red with shock
And I tried to laugh along with them
Wishing they would stop.

For those flowing feathery things
That I thought were really wings
With which a goldfish swims
Are fins, are fins, are fins.

The Moving Stair

The first time I went to Limerick
We went into this big store:
They had tons of things for grown-
ups
On the bottom floor.

And Mammy went to sample
All sorts of perfume there,
When just below the counter
I saw this moving stair.

So I jumped up on it
With a spaceman kind of hop,
And up, up, up I floated—
But the stair just wouldn't stop.

And then when I had gotten up,
I felt a proper clown—
For the stair just kept on moving.
How *was* I to get down?

And then it dawned upon me
That I was alone and lost,
And I was small and frightened,
And Mammy would be cross.

So then, I suppose you've guessed it—
I let out such a roar
That Mammy dropped the perfume
Down on the bottom floor.

And Mammy—she came for me
And I wasn't lost at all,
But that was quite a while ago
When I was young and small.

Better Than You...

I'm better than you at school.
You're not—I'm better than you.

Well anyway, my mother knows
more than your mother.
She doesn't—my mother knows more
than yours.

She doesn't—my mother is older than
your mother.
She's not—my mother is older than
yours.

Well anyway, my mother has more
grey hairs than your mother.
Yeah—but my mother's cheeks are
softer than yours.

Well, my mother has false teeth and your mother hasn't.
She has—and my mother has glasses too.

I don't care—my mother knows more than your mother.
She doesn't—I'm better than you at school...

A Winter-Feed for the Birds

Birds chirped in my back garden
Feeding from the plate.
I watched them from my window
But the chirping of a gate

Frightened them. Away they flew
Till the stranger came indoors:
Then they hopped back to the garden
In twos and threes and fours.

Warily they stabbed their food,
Watching all around
For anything that shouldn't be,
For any foreign sound.

Thrush bullied tit and wren;
Blackbird bullied thrush;
Till crow zoomed in and scattered all
To every barren bush.

Crow scattered crumbs and ate his fill
And flapped away again;
And then came puffy bullfinch,
Red robin and stubby wren.

I'd Like to Be a Garage Man

I'd like to be a garage man
And work with gears and wires.
I'd quickly fix your punctures
And change your worn-out tyres.

I'd fix your car and spray it—
I'd make it look like new.
And then I'd drive and test it
To make it safe for you.

Oh, I'd be happy working
Down in the black pit
Changing oil and tightening nuts,
My hair and face all grit.

When I leave school and I am big
I want no plane nor carriage—
I'll drive the biggest, fastest car
When I have my own garage.

Driving Lesson

"Why'd you bring that car to school?"
—Just hear the teacher bawl.
I brought my car to school today
To drive him up the wall!

An Only Child
For Aoife Byrne

Oh, they'll say you're pampered,
And they'll say you're spoiled,
But *I'll* tell you one thing—
It isn't easy being an only child.

When you've brothers and sisters
You're never alone,
But who's going to play with me
When *I'm* at home?

And when Mam and Dad are cross at
me
I get all the blame—
I've no brothers or sisters
To share the pain.

I suppose, to be honest
I have more toys
Than many of the other
Girls and boys.

But I wish I had a brother
Or a sister, or both:
Life would be much better fun
And that's the truth.

I Wish That Rain Was Sweets

I wish that rain was sweets!
How lovely it would be
To gather sweets in bucketfuls
For breakfast, dinner, tea.

I wish the rain was sweets—
Blue ones, green ones, red:
A rainbow full of magic sweets
In the sky above my head.

I wish the rain was sweets—
But Mammy says to me
That if I got all the sweets I want
I couldn't have my tea:

But I wouldn't mind, you see!

The Jackdaws in the Schoolyard

The jackdaws in the schoolyard
Forage every day
For crumbs and crisps and sandwich-
ends
When we've finished play.

They perch upon the chimneys,
On every tree and bush;
They land and peck the schoolyard
Then fly off with a whoosh.

I wish I was a jackdaw
With quick and beady eye:
I'd never have to go to school—
I'd live up in the sky.

I'd get my food in schoolyards,
From bins and rubbish-heaps;
And my friends and I would roost at
night
And sing ourselves to sleep.

The Chase

Once I maddened Mammy
—That's not so hard to do,
But this time I really got her:
She chased me—off I flew;

She chased and chased, but I'm too
fit—
I raced her till she stopped;
Then safe, the house between us,
I halted. Soon I popped

My head around the gable
And sweetly called "Cuckoo"
Till Mammy smiled—all would be
well
In an hour or two.

I Wish I Had a Broomstick

I wish I had a broomstick
To fly up in the air.
Oh, I wish I had a broomstick
To go zooming everywhere.

Though Mammy says there's no such
thing,
I don't believe a word.
If only I had a broomstick
I'd fly faster than a bird.

Over houses, over hills,
Way up in the sky.
If I had a broomstick
I'd fly and fly and fly.

The Garden

My big brother's
Such a cissy,
Combs his hair
And always prissy;

Always bossing
Me around—
"Do this! Do that!
Don't make a sound!"

He got a garden
Full of flowers,
He planted them—
It took him hours

Of sowing, weeding
—All that stuff—
And now my brother's
In a huff

'Cos his flowers
No longer grow.
Who pulled them up?
Well...I dunno—

But he bossed me
Once too much
And now his garden's
Growing scutch...

The Best Pussykitten in Moybane
In memoriam Tom Fitzmaurice

Tom is dead
My Daddy says
He's gone to heaven

I wonder what he's like
Heaven
From what Daddy says
I'd say he's nice

Tom is dead
He can't walk any more
I wonder can he walk in Heaven

We all went to Tom's *hopsital*
To see him

Mammy said that I was good
In *hopsital*
Tom didn't talk
And he had no fags
Mary spoke to him
And held his hand

Tom is dead
My Daddy says

He's not in *hopsital* any more

He had a funeral

Daddy always puts on his suit
At funerals
And comes home late

He sleeps with me
If I'm still awake
When he comes home

John likes that
I like to pull his hair
When I'm going to sleep

My Daddy is a pussy cat
And I'm his baby kitten
Granda says I'm the best pussykitten
In Moybane

I wonder why Tom
Doesn't come to John's house
Any more

Big Mouth

"How would you like your head broken?
How would you like another tooth knocked
out?
Be careful or I'll flatten you,"
Says Big Mouth.

"No I wouldn't like my head broken
And anyway my first tooth fell out,
You couldn't flatten me that easy,
Big Mouth!"

Christmas Morning

Santa's toys
Were on the floor
When I got up at six
Or half past four;

And Mam and Dad
Were still in bed
But I was not
A sleepyhead:

In my new car
I was a winner;
Then Mam got up
And put on the dinner:

And I raced myself
Down through the hall—
Driver, engine,
Crowd and all

Till Mam called out
"Dinner's up! Come on!"
And I still had my
Pyjamas on.

Don't

Daddy's full of
"Don't do that..."
"Don't spill the milk!
Don't kick the cat!

Don't run! Don't stop!
Don't climb! Don't fall!"
I don't know what
To do at all.

Because I *can*
He tells me "Don't,"
But will I stop?
Of course I won't!

Bells

I wonder what a bell says:
What is its special call?
Though everyone says it's "ding-
dong,"
It's not ding-dong at all.

Because every bell is different—
Bells boom and clang and bleep,
Bells buzz and chime and tinkle,
They alarm you from your sleep.

Mostly bells are not too bad,
But there's one that sure annoys:
It's the school bell that ends playtime
For us, poor girls and boys.

The Robin in the Woods

Margie, Brenda
Brian and I
Saw a robin
In the sky

Flying up
Among the trees,
Rejoicing in
The spring's first breeze.

And then she flew
Without a sound
Down beside us
On the ground

And hopped and stopped
Without a tweet
In the mossy wood
About our feet.

Mostly
The birds I see,
Suspecting humans,
Are afraid of me;

But this perky bird
So brave and small
Was not afraid
At all, at all.

Pension Day

Nan brought me to the village
To get her pension paid,
Then she brought me to the pub
To get some lemonade—

At least that's how she said it:
She bought a pot of tea
And crisps and buns and
doughnuts—
And lemonade for me.

After we had finished
I said I'd like to play
A game of pool with Nana
(I always get my way

With Nana);
So we started to play pool
And Nana had to put me
Standing on a stool

So I could see the pool-balls.
I beat them with the pole
Then stood up on the table
And kicked them in the hole.

And then we went for shopping—
Something for our tea:
Cake and buns for Nana,
Lemonade for me.

The Mam

Evenings when I was very small
I always clutched a stick
To save myself from the monstrous
Mam—
She really scared me stiff.

With a brown coat
And a big brown hat
And a big brown message-bag
And a face that was neither snarl nor
smile,
She scared me, that old hag.

And always about tea-time
My stick would go BANG! BANG!
As I beat the step outside our door
To keep away the Mam.

And Mammy used to ask me
Why I got so awful mad;
Then I'd promise not to kill her—
I'd just scare that wizened hag.
With a big brown coat
And a big brown hat
And a big brown message-bag
And a face that was neither snarl
nor smile,
She scared me, that old hag.

But now I'm a little older
And a bit more sensible,
And now I know for certain
She was not a hag at all

But a tired old tattered woman
Astray in mind and limb
And I'm sorry that my terror
Made me do such frightful things.

But the big brown coat
And the big brown hat
And the big brown message-bag
And the face that was neither snarl
nor smile
Would scare a little lad.

The Boody Man

For Lucy, Amy and Rory Kiberd

Before the mountains and the sea,
Before the sky began
The void sang forth its harmony.
Then came the Boody Man.

He had a bag for boys like me
To steal us from our play—
Behind each smile, behind each laugh
He was never far away.

He lived this side of nightmare,
I knew, at Buckley's gate,
And, as night fell, the Boody Man
Would lurk and lie in wait.

Young scallywags at nightfall
Would trick him with a plan—
They ducked behind the Creamery wall
And ran and ran and ran.

But once as I was passing
From the village late,
I peeped and saw a couple
Kissing at the gate.

The Boody Man had vanished
Back where he began—
One lively look had banished him
As only childhood can.

Also by Poolbeg

Mouse and the Lemon Boy

By

Tony Hickey

Mouse and the Lemon Boy live in the middle of a shop window.

Mouse is made of marshmallow and is a pretty pink colour. The Lemon Boy is made of lemon candy and is bright yellow. They get tired of sitting in a shop window waiting for a child to buy them.

One quiet Sunday they set off on their adventures through the streets of the town. They meet ducks, dogs, some nice children and some naughty ones. They have some enjoyable adventures and some frightening ones before they eventually return by bus to the safety of their shop window. The text includes the words and music of the songs they learn on their travels.